AMERICAN SPACE MISSIONS
ASTRONAUTS, EXPLORATION, AND DISCOVERY

D0103043

Danger in Space
Surviving the Apollo 13 Disaster

Henry M. Holden

Enslow Publishers, Inc.
40 Industrial Road
Box 398
Berkeley Heights, NJ 07922
USA

http://www.enslow.com

Original edition published as *Triumph Over Disaster Aboard* Apollo 13 in 2004.

Library of Congress Cataloging-in-Publication Data

Holden, Henry M.
  Danger in space : surviving the Apollo 13 disaster / Henry M. Holden.
    p. cm. — (American space missions—astronauts, exploration, and discovery)
  Originally published: Triumph over disaster aboard Apollo 13, 2004.
  Includes bibliographical references and index.
  Summary: "Explores the Apollo 13 mission, including the causes of the disaster aboard the spacecraft, how the astronauts
fixed the problems, and how the crew were saved"—Provided by publisher.
  Audience: Grades 4–6.
  ISBN 978-0-7660-4072-4
  1. Apollo 13 (Spacecraft)—Juvenile literature. 2. Project Apollo (U.S.)—Juvenile literature. 3. Space vehicle accidents—
United States—Juvenile literature. I. Title.
  TL789.8.U6A5415 2013
  629.45'4—dc23
                          2011037734

Future editions:
Paperback ISBN 978-1-4644-0073-5
ePUB ISBN 978-1-4645-0980-3
PDF ISBN 978-1-4646-0980-0

Printed in the United States of America

032012 Lake Book Manufacturing, Inc., Melrose Park, IL

10 9 8 7 6 5 4 3 2 1

To Our Readers: We have done our best to make sure all Internet addresses in this book were active and appropriate
when we went to press. However, the author and the publisher have no control over and assume no liability for the material
available on those Internet sites or on other Web sites they may link to. Any comments or suggestions can be sent by e-mail
to comments@enslow.com or to the address on the back cover.

♻ Enslow Publishers, Inc., is committed to printing our books on recycled paper. The paper in every book contains 10% to
30% post-consumer waste (PCW). The cover board on the outside of each book contains 100% PCW. Our goal is to do our
part to help young people and the environment too!

Illustration Credits: AP Images, p. 30; AP Images / J. Spencer Jones, p. 35; Everett Collection, p. 41; Mark Paternostro
/ Photo Researchers, Inc., p. 14; NASA, pp. 1, 4, 8, 11, 13, 20, 23, 25, 26, 29, 32, 37, 39; NASA Headquarters, p. 7; NASA
History Office, p. 17; NASA Johnson Space Center, p. 19.

Cover Illustration: David A. Hardy / Photo Researchers, Inc. (Artist's rendering of the explosion on *Apollo 13*).

Contents

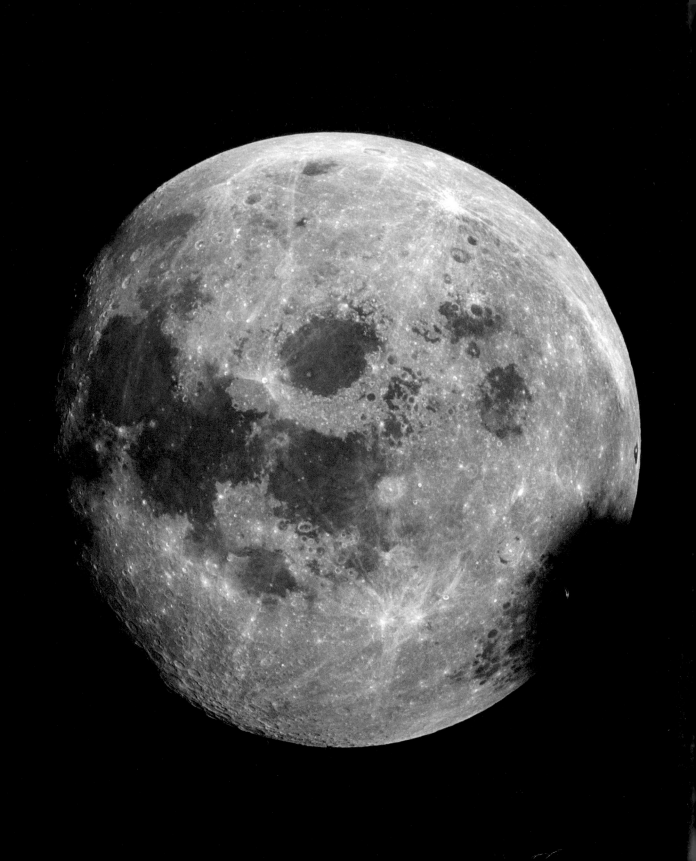

CHAPTER 1

Danger and Disaster

It was April 11, 1970. Astronauts James A. Lovell, Jr., John (Jack) L. Swigert, Jr., and Fred W. Haise, Jr., were rocketing toward the Moon at 25,000 miles (40,225 kilometers) per hour. *Apollo 13* was going faster than a bullet! The National Aeronautics and Space Administration (NASA) was sending this spacecraft to Fra Mauro, a range of hills on the Moon. The astronauts were going to collect rock samples so scientists could learn more about the Moon.

Apollo 13 looked like a perfect flight. The people in Mission Control started to relax but remained alert.[1] About forty-six hours into the flight, Joe Kerwin, the capsule communicator (CapCom) on duty, said, "The spacecraft is in real good shape. . . .We're bored to tears down here."[2] A few hours later, the boredom would end suddenly. The situation would turn into a life-and-death struggle in outer space.

Explosion on Board

On April 13, almost fifty-six hours into the mission, the crew began a television broadcast from the command module. Mission Control in Houston played music for the astronauts. It included the song "Aquarius" and the theme from the movie *2001, A Space Odyssey*. The television broadcast ended with Lovell saying, "This is the crew of *Apollo 13* wishing everybody there a nice evening. . . ."[3]

A few minutes later, a system light indicated low pressure in one of the fuel tanks. Houston asked the astronauts to do a cryogenic stir. They would stir the super-cold oxygen and hydrogen with remote fans. This would raise the pressure. About sixteen seconds later, the crew heard a loud bang. Swigert, strapped in his seat, felt a strong vibration. Lovell, floating in the command module, felt the noise rumble through him. Haise, who was in the tunnel between the command module and the lunar module, saw the walls move around him.[4] This was Swigert's and Haise's first spaceflight. Lovell thought Haise had opened a valve. He turned toward Haise. What he saw were the eyes of someone who was frightened.[5] Haise had not opened a valve. What happened was not something their training had covered. This was Lovell's fourth trip into space, but this was something he had not experienced before.

"Houston—We've Had a Problem"

Swigert calmly reported, "Okay, Houston, we've had a problem here."[6] Jack Lousma was the CapCom on duty. "This is Houston," said Lousma. "Say again, please." Lovell came on the radio. "Houston, we've had a problem." His voice was calm, but his heart was beating faster.[7] He reported they had a "main B bus undervolt." This meant they were losing power in one of the three fuel cells.

An alarm was sounding in the astronauts' headsets. Other warning lights lit up the panel, showing that two of the three fuel cells were dead. These were the spacecraft's primary source of electricity. The warning lights also showed one oxygen tank was completely empty. There were signs that the other tank was losing oxygen rapidly. Something had gone terribly wrong on *Apollo 13*.

A view of Mission Control Center in Houston, Texas, on April 13, 1970, during the video transmission from *Apollo 13*. The television screen at the top of the image shows astronaut Fred W. Haise, Jr. Moments after the live broadcast ended, an explosion occurred on the spacecraft.

This is an artist's rendering of the lunar module from *Apollo 13* descending toward the Moon's surface. Unfortunately, the *Apollo 13* astronauts never did get to land on the Moon. After the explosion in the oxygen tank, their only goal was to return to Earth safely.

Losing Oxygen

Houston figured out that there had been an explosion in the service module (SM) attached to the capsule. Thirteen minutes after the explosion, Lovell looked out the left-hand window. What he saw made him realize they were facing a potential disaster. "We are venting something out into the—into space," said Lovell, "it looks like a gas."[8] It was oxygen escaping at a high rate from the second, and last, oxygen tank. The escaping gas was causing the spacecraft to pitch and roll, and Lovell fought to keep it under control.[9]

Apollo 13 was more than 200,000 miles (321,800 kilometers) from Earth and about 45,000 miles (72,405 kilometers) from the gray, pockmarked surface of the Moon. It was just entering the Moon's gravitational pull. The spacecraft did not have enough power to turn back, and an emergency landing on the Moon was out of the question. One science reporter predicted the crew had about a 10 percent chance of making it home alive.[10] The world held its breath, while the engineers in Houston worked to save the lives of the three astronauts.

CHAPTER 2

Liftoff

Apollo 13 was the third mission to attempt to land on the Moon. As always, great care was taken in preparing for the space mission. The astronauts trained for months and planned for every possible emergency. At the end of their training, they felt they were ready for almost anything. Teams of thousands on the ground would be backing them up. Mission Control is always aware that once a rocket is launched, there is little anyone on the ground can do if things should happen to go wrong.

The Age of *Aquarius*

The Saturn V rocket lifted the command-service module, *Odyssey*, off the launchpad at Cape Canaveral. The command module contains the crew compartment, controls, many of the spacecraft's systems, and the heat shield. The service module, attached to the command module, contains the propulsion system and the oxygen and hydrogen fuel.

The Saturn V rocket ignites, lifting *Apollo 13* off the launchpad at Cape Canaveral, Florida, on April 11, 1970. This was NASA's third mission to attempt a moon landing.

Inside the rocket is the lunar module *Aquarius*. The lunar module is the only part of the spacecraft that lands on the Moon.

The five engines of the second stage of the rocket ignited and burned smoothly for about five minutes. The crew felt a strong vibration, and then the center engine unexpectedly shut down two minutes early. The engineers in Houston fired the remaining four engines thirty-four seconds longer than planned. This would make up for the lost thrust. The third stage would burn for nine extra seconds to put them in Earth orbit. "We heaved sighs of relief, thinking we had gotten through what probably would be the one major glitch in the mission," said Eugene Kranz, the mission's chief flight director.[1] There was no hint of the great danger ahead.

Docking With *Aquarius*

Two hours later, the rocket's third stage fired again. *Odyssey* broke out of Earth orbit and was on a course to the Moon. It would take about three days to reach the Moon. About an hour later, Jack Swigert, the command module pilot, separated the command module from the third stage of the rocket. Swigert turned *Odyssey* around and docked with *Aquarius*. Then, easing the lunar module from the rocket, the two vehicles headed for the Moon.

Jack Swigert had originally been the backup pilot on *Apollo 13*. When command module pilot Thomas Ken Mattingly was exposed to rubella (German measles), Swigert replaced him. Swigert had some

James Lovell (left), Jack Swigert (center), and Fred Haise pose for a photograph before the launch of *Apollo 13*.

previous experience. He had been a member of the support crew for the *Apollo 7* mission.

Fred Haise was the lunar module pilot. He had been a research pilot at NASA and a Marines fighter pilot. He was a backup lunar module pilot for the *Apollo 8* and the *Apollo 11* missions.

Captain James A. Lovell was the spacecraft commander. He was the most experienced of the crew. "I had never felt more confident. On my three previous missions, I had already logged 572 hours in space. . . ."[2] Lovell flew on *Gemini 7* and commanded the *Gemini 12* mission. Lovell was also the command module pilot on *Apollo 8*, America's first voyage to the Moon.

The spacecraft's name would ironically foretell its adventure. Lovell named the spacecraft *Odyssey* because it means "a long voyage marked by many changes of fortune." He named the lunar module after Aquarius, the water carrier of Egyptian mythology.[3]

Stages of the Lunar Module

Both Lovell and Haise would ride the lunar module to the surface of the Moon. There are two stages to the lunar module. The descent stage

This illustration shows the oxygen tank in the service module exploding during the *Apollo 13* mission. After the blast, the three astronauts and NASA scientists at Mission Control had to come up with a plan to save the crew before oxygen ran out in the command module.

holds the fuel, and the descent engine is used to land on the Moon. The astronauts return to the command module using the ascent stage. This stage has three sections: the crew compartment, the midsection, and the aft equipment bay. Only the crew compartment and midsection are pressurized. It also has an engine to lift it off the Moon. The crew compartment is about 8 feet (2.4 meters) wide and 42 inches (106.7 centimeters) deep. A tunnel ring on the top of the ascent stage connects it to the command module. The 32-inch-wide (81.2 centimeters) docking tunnel extends down into the midsection. The crew uses this tunnel to move between the command module and the lunar module.[4]

Lunar Lifeboat

Nothing like this had ever happened before. Even before the crew discovered the oxygen leak, they tried to close the hatch between the command module and the lunar module. "We reacted spontaneously, like submarine crews, closing the hatches to limit the amount of flooding," Lovell said.[5]

The explosion had damaged most of the command module's electrical systems. The lunar module had not been damaged. One hour after the explosion, CapCom Jack Lousma said, "It (oxygen) is slowly going to zero, and we are starting to think about the LM lifeboat." Swigert replied, "That's what we have been thinking about too."[6] What they were thinking had never been tried.

CHAPTER 3

Saving the Crew

It took about fifteen minutes for Houston to realize that the crew was in grave danger. After things sank in, Central Command began to understand the enormous crisis before them. "Once we understood it, we realized that there was not going to be a lunar mission," said Eugene Kranz. "The mission had become one of survival."[1]

Bringing the astronauts home safely would be a challenge. The crew knew they were in serious trouble. "The debris around the spacecraft was tremendous," said Lovell. "There was so much debris all around outside the spacecraft; we couldn't even see stars."[2] The explosion had blown away one of the two liquid oxygen tanks on the service module. The remaining tank was losing oxygen into space and would soon be empty. When that happened, there would be no oxygen for the crew to breathe. *Odyssey* was, in essence, bleeding to death.

The astronauts could not remain in the damaged command module. Houston decided the lunar module would have to act as a lifeboat. It could support two astronauts for about two days on the Moon. It had

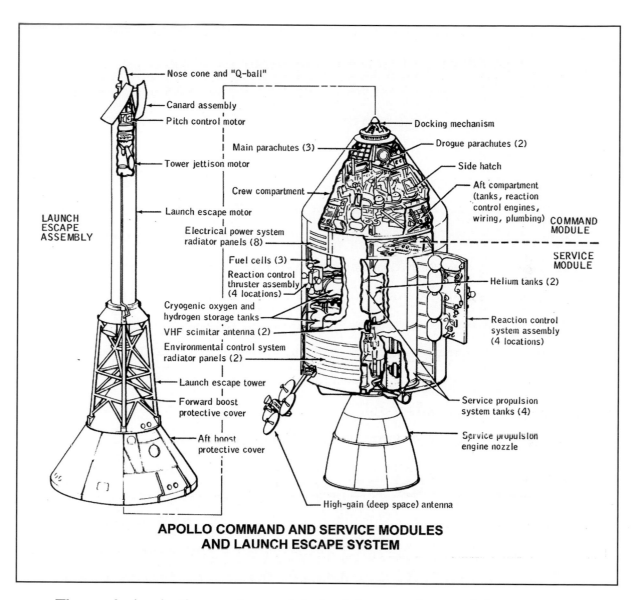

Nose cone and "Q-ball"

Canard assembly

Pitch control motor

Main parachutes (3)

Tower jettison motor

Crew compartment

Launch escape motor

LAUNCH
ESCAPE
ASSEMBLY

Electrical power system
radiator panels (8)

Fuel cells (3)

Reaction control
thruster assembly
(4 locations)

Cryogenic oxygen and
hydrogen storage tanks

VHF scimitar antenna (2)

Environmental control system
radiator panels (2)

Launch escape tower

Forward boost
protective cover

Aft boost
protective cover

Docking mechanism

Drogue parachutes (2)

Side hatch

Aft compartment
(tanks, reaction
control engines,
wiring, plumbing) COMMAND
MODULE

SERVICE
MODULE

Helium tanks (2)

Reaction control
system assembly
(4 locations)

Service propulsion
system tanks (4)

Service propulsion
engine nozzle

High-gain (deep space) antenna

**APOLLO COMMAND AND SERVICE MODULES
AND LAUNCH ESCAPE SYSTEM**

The explosion in the service module had destroyed one of the oxygen
tanks and caused the other one to leak. If the crew remained in the
command module when the oxygen tank emptied, they would die.
This is a diagram of the *Apollo* command and service modules.

oxygen and an engine. However, there were three crew members, and they were about four days from Earth.[3] There was no choice if the crew were to stay alive until Houston could figure out what to do. *Odyssey* had only fifteen minutes of power left.[4] Kranz ordered the crew to shut down *Odyssey* and climb into the lunar module. It was a race to see if the crew could get *Aquarius* powered up in time.

Houston faced a difficult task. A coast-to-coast network of simulators, computers, astronauts, and manufacturers of the spacecraft was hooked up with Houston. New procedures had to be written for the emergency. Ken Mattingly was in the command module simulator. He would test the procedures in the simulator before they were passed up to the crew.[5]

The command module was the only spacecraft that could get the crew back to Earth. It had a heat shield to protect them from the three thousand degrees (1,648.9°C) of reentry heat. However, the heat shield side of the command module was joined to the service module. No one knew if the shield was damaged from the explosion.

Failure Is Not an Option

NASA had never faced a problem like this before. However, they did have about ten years experience with sending men into space. They also had time. It would take several days for the spacecraft to loop around the Moon and head back to Earth. "These three astronauts were beyond our physical reach," said Kranz. "But, not beyond the reach of human imagination, inventiveness, and a creed that we all lived by: 'Failure is not an option.'"[6]

A view of the service module after the explosion shows an entire panel blown away. **NASA** had never faced a problem like this before. They did not know if the lunar module had enough power to get the crew back to Earth or if the command module's heat shield could protect them upon reentry.

Staying Alive

There were many things to do. "It turned out that we had enough oxygen," said Lovell.[7] They were not so sure about the power. "A quick estimate . . . left us at least thirty-six hours short on battery power," said Kranz.[8] He later revised the figure. They were twenty-four hours short on power and thirty-six hours short on water for the return trip.[9] They could not use the remaining battery power on *Odyssey*. It was needed for reentry. "We thought that was enough (power) if we turned off every electrical power device not absolutely necessary," said Lovell.[10]

Cooling water was a major problem. The crew would run out of water before they got home. The fuel cells mix liquid hydrogen and

This photo taken by the crew of *Apollo 13* shows the farside of the Moon. When the spacecraft flew behind the Moon, Jack Swigert and Fred Haise took many photographs. Unlike James Lovell, the two astronauts had not been on a mission to the Moon before.

oxygen to make electricity and water. The water is used to cool the equipment and for the astronauts to drink. The astronauts cut their water down to six ounces (177.4 milliliters) each per day. They drank what fruit juices they had and ate hot dogs and the wet-pack foods. They had no hot water so they could not eat the freeze-dried foods.[11] By the fourth day, the astronauts were severely dehydrated.

Going Home

In order to get the crew home safely, the damaged *Apollo 13* would have to loop around the Moon like a boomerang. Before the explosion, they had made a normal course correction that would put them on course to land on the Moon. Now they had to fire their engine before looping around the Moon to put them on a "free return trajectory to Earth."[12] When they flew around the farside, lunar gravity would slingshot them homeward bound.

When *Apollo 13* flew behind the Moon, they were so close that the craters and mountains filled the windows. "I was busy running down the procedures," said Lovell. "Suddenly, I noticed that Swigert and Haise had their cameras out and were busy photographing the lunar surface. 'If we don't make this next maneuver correctly, you won't get your pictures developed!'" said Lovell.[13] They said, "'Relax, Jim, you've already been here before, but we haven't.'"[14]

During the next twenty-eight minutes, the Moon would block all communications between Houston and the crew.[15] Houston would not know if anything went wrong.

CHAPTER 4

The Long Journey Home

The radio in Houston crackled with static. Then, a voice came through the speaker: "Houston, *Aquarius*. . . . The view out there is fantastic. . . ."[1] *Apollo 13* was on its way home. Still, it would take more than three days to get the astronauts home safely. The plan was to fire the engine on *Aquarius* to get them home before their water and battery power ran out. However, the lunar module engine had not been designed to push the command module.

Heading Home

Setting an accurate course for the return trip home would also be difficult. The explosion had damaged the command module's navigation system. They were traveling in a vacuum, and the debris from the explosion traveled with them. The sunlight reflecting off the debris made navigation impossible. With the debris blocking the stars, they could not align the command module for reentry. With help from

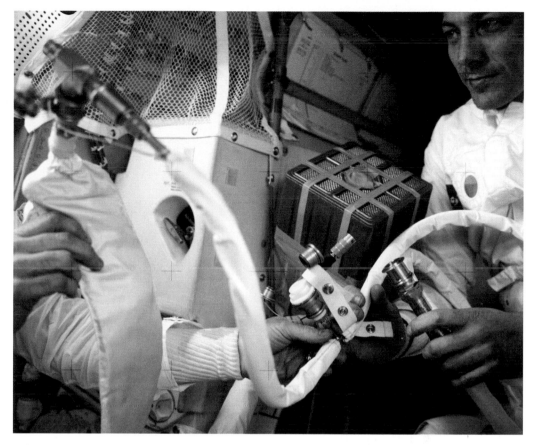

After *Apollo 13* went around the Moon, the astronauts needed to use the engine on *Aquarius* to get them home before their water and battery power ran out. Jack Swigert was in charge of starting and stopping the engine. In this photo inside the lunar module, Swigert (right) uses the feed water bag.

Mission Control, the crew used the sun and the crescent shape of Earth to confirm their flight path. The Sun's large diameter, however, could result in great error, but no one had a better plan.

Two hours after *Apollo 13* emerged from behind the Moon, it was time to fire the lunar module engine. Swigert watched the timer. He would signal when to start and stop the burn.[2] Lovell flipped the switch that fired the engine in *Aquarius*. There was no sound from the engine. The only way they knew the engine was burning was the sensation they had of being pushed toward the floor of the ship. The burn had to be precise. If it were too short, the craft would skip off Earth's atmosphere, like a stone skimming over water. If it were too long, the craft would burn up entering the atmosphere. The two men controlled the burn manually for four and a half minutes. The burn was perfect.[3] Houston gave them the good news. *Apollo 13* would arrive back to Earth about ten hours earlier than originally planned.

Still, Houston had serious concerns about the crew's safety. No one knew how long the damaged service module would last. They had used more power during the second burn. Now they would have to power down *Aquarius* if they were to make it home. In addition, *Aquarius* was getting cold. It had been twenty-six hours since part of the service module had exploded, and the crew had not gotten any sleep.[4]

Round Peg in a Square Hole

After a day and a half in *Aquarius*, a warning light showed the carbon dioxide was at a dangerous level. On Earth, we breathe in oxygen and breathe out carbon dioxide. Green plants convert the carbon dioxide back into oxygen. There were no green plants on *Apollo 13*, but oxygen was not the problem. The astronauts' breathing out was the problem. Their breathing was slowly poisoning the air with carbon dioxide.

On a normal flight, special filters trap the carbon dioxide in canisters. The round canisters in *Aquarius* would not last long enough

A photo of Earth taken from *Apollo 13* during its journey home. The astronauts had to use the engine burn perfectly. If they did not, the spacecraft could skip off Earth's atmosphere, or it could burn up after reentry.

This is an interior view of the lunar module during the *Apollo 13* return flight. It shows the contraption that the astronauts constructed with cardboard, plastic bags, a sock, and duct tape in order to filter out carbon dioxide from the spacecraft. If NASA engineers had not come up with this design, the astronauts would have died from carbon dioxide poisoning.

to get the astronauts home. The square canisters in *Odyssey* would not fit in *Aquarius*. "We would have died of the exhaust from our own lungs if Mission Control hadn't come up with a marvelous fix," Lovell said.[5]

Engineers had figured out a way to attach a canister from *Odyssey* to the *Aquarius* system. They used plastic bags, cardboard, a sock, and duct tape. These were all materials that the crew had on board the spacecraft.[6] "Jack (Swigert) and I put it together: just like building a model airplane,"[7] Lovell said.

Inside the capsule, it was cold. To save power, the crew shut down most electrical systems. In the darkened spacecraft, the temperature dropped to 38°F (3.3°C), just a little above freezing. There were no blankets or warm clothes on board. Lovell and Haise put on their lunar boots; Swigert wore an extra suit of underwear. Water condensed on the cabin walls, and the windows frosted. Sleep was almost impossible because of the cold. "We were as cold as frogs in a frozen pool, especially Jack Swigert, who got his feet wet and didn't have lunar overshoes,"[8] said Lovell. The astronauts thought about putting on their space suits, but they were bulky and would make them sweat. Houston was concerned that any movement in the spacecraft might disturb its flight path. "We longed for some good old thermal underwear," said Lovell.[9]

Attention had been on keeping the crew alive and getting the wounded spacecraft home. However, Houston saw another serious problem. *Apollo 13* was off course.

CHAPTER 5

Preparation for Reentry

Something was pushing *Apollo 13* away from Earth. Houston calculated that it would miss Earth by 99 miles (158.7 kilometers). Gas was escaping from somewhere on the spacecraft.[1] Gravity was pulling *Apollo 13* faster toward Earth. This was good news for the astronauts. Still, if they did not fire the lunar module engine again, they would orbit Earth forever.[2] Before the crew cut the service module loose, they fired the lunar module engine one last time. This put the spacecraft on the course needed to enter the atmosphere.

Return to *Odyssey*

The astronauts had been in the lunar module for four days and nights. For reentry, they would have to return to *Odyssey*, which had the heat shield to protect the crew upon reentry. However, *Odyssey* did not have

In this photo, Fred Haise goes through simulation training before the *Apollo 13* mission. Although the astronauts had never dealt with this disastrous situation before, their rigorous training had prepared them to be ready for anything in space.

On April 17, shortly before reentering Earth's atmosphere, the crew released the service module. In order to help NASA engineers figure out what had caused the explosion, the astronauts took photographs of the service module as it floated away.

enough power. The battery in the command module needed full power to reenter the atmosphere successfully. On Thursday morning, Swigert began transferring the remaining power in *Aquarius* to the battery in *Odyssey*.

No one in Houston knew if the heat shield and the command module would hold up under the force of reentry. On Friday, April 17, about four hours before *Apollo 13* was to reenter the atmosphere, the crew released the service module. Houston had insisted on keeping it until the last minute. No one knew what the cold in space might do to the unprotected heat shield. If it was damaged, it could not be fixed. It would mean certain death for the crew on reentry.

The astronauts watched the damaged module float away. They took photographs hoping that they might be able to help figure out what had happened eighty-two hours earlier. The explosion had been a large one. The crew could see pieces of insulation, broken wires, and a charred black hole where the oxygen tank had been. "I'm glad we weren't able to see the SM earlier. With one whole panel missing, and wreckage hanging out, it was a sorry mess as it drifted away," Lovell said later.[3]

About three hours later, the crew opened the hatch and floated from *Aquarius* into the command module. When the crew entered *Odyssey*, they found the walls, ceiling, floor, and panels all covered with droplets of water. They wondered if the water would cause electrical short circuits and perhaps a fire.

Slowly, one system at a time, they powered up the command module. There were no short circuits, and everything was working. They closed

This photo shows the lunar module after the astronauts released it into space. The "lifeboat" had saved their lives.

the hatch between *Aquarius* and *Odyssey* and flipped a switch. The lunar module blasted away from the command module. The fragile *Aquarius*, without a heat shield, would burn up in the atmosphere.

"Farewell, *Aquarius*, and we thank you," said Houston. "She was a good ship," Lovell added. Astronaut Alan Bean had said, "Once the lunar module has blown away . . . the reentry will be about the same as on any other mission, and the emergency will be essentially over."[4] Still, everyone wondered if the heat shield would hold.

The doctors also worried that the crew members were so tired that they would make critical mistakes. They had traveled more than a half million miles (804,500 kilometers). They were almost home, but one mistake could cause disaster. The officials in Houston hoped they could hang on for a few more hours.

Apollo 13 had roared into space on top of a twenty-eight-story Saturn rocket. The 51,000-pound (23,133.6-kilogram) service module and the 23-foot (7-meter) lunar module that had kept them alive for four days were gone.[5] All that was left was the 11-foot-tall (3.4-meter) bell-shaped capsule tearing through space on a nonstop, one-way trip toward Earth.

CHAPTER 6

Reentry

Just before the normal three-minute radio blackout that occurs during reentry, Jack Swigert said to Houston, "I know all of us here want to thank all you guys down there for the very fine job you did."[1] *Apollo 13*'s speed rose quickly as it angled earthward. Earth's gravity was pulling them home. The spacecraft was traveling more than 25,000 miles (40,225 kilometers) per hour when it plunged into the atmosphere.[2] As it entered the atmosphere, the friction began to heat the command module. Some of the heat shield is designed to burn away as the command module falls toward Earth. No one knew if the shield would withstand the three thousand degrees (1,648.9°C) of reentry heat. No one wanted to think about what would happen if it did not. After all the crew had survived, there was still a danger of their burning up on reentry.

The crew watched Earth grow larger and larger in their windows. Swigert looked out the left-hand window. Haise looked out the right, and Lovell peered out the center window. First, there was a slight sense of gravity returning, and then a pink glow appeared in the windows.

An enormous crowd at Grand Central Station in New York City watches a large television screen waiting for the safe splashdown of *Apollo 13*.

The glow turned orange, and then red flames filled the windows. The energy in the fire was enough to light the city of Los Angeles for more than one minute.[3] In Houston, the only sound from the radio was static.

A Successful Failure

Three minutes went by. There was dead silence in the control room. Anxiously, everyone watched the large screen overhead. There were color television cameras aboard the aircraft carrier USS *Iwo Jima* and in a helicopter in the recovery area. The morning was clear, and the sea was calm. People around the world watched and listened. They hoped they would hear the astronauts' voices and see the spacecraft drift down through the clouds.

"*Odyssey*, Houston standing by." Four minutes went by, and there was still nothing on the radio except static. Mission Control should have heard from the crew by now. There was a sinking feeling in the control room.[4] They called again and again. Then, over the radio came two words. "Okay, Joe." It was Jack Swigert. Everyone in Houston breathed a sigh of relief. "We read you, Jack," came the response.[5]

Still, no one could breathe easy. They wondered if the electronics used to deploy the parachutes would work. Minutes went by and then, at 24,000 feet, *Odyssey*'s three orange-and-white main chutes appeared. *Apollo 13* splashed down in the ocean. The crew was safe. Cheers and applause erupted in the control room. Rescue swimmers jumped from a helicopter, attached a flotation collar to the capsule, and opened the hatch. The crew members crawled out and into rubber life rafts. From the rafts, they were each hoisted to the recovery helicopter.

On board the aircraft carrier *Iwo Jima*, doctors examined the crew. They were tired, hungry, and dehydrated. They had not washed for days. Lovell had lost fourteen pounds (6.4 kilograms), and Haise and Swigert another seventeen pounds (7.7 kilograms) between them. The crew set a record by losing a total of almost thirty-two pounds (14.5 kilograms), nearly 50 percent more than any other crew had lost.[6] Haise had developed a urinary infection and a high fever. He was seriously ill for three weeks.

The aborted *Apollo 13* mission was technically a failure. It was the first in twenty-two manned flights that a mission did not achieve its objectives. However, the experience gained in rescuing the crew made

The crew of *Apollo 13* (left) sit in a raft outside the command module waiting for the recovery helicopter to take them to the **USS** *Iwo Jima* after their successful splashdown.

it a "successful failure." The key to its success was that no one thought about failure. No one believed the crew would be lost. "Throughout the entire mission I had believed in my heart that we would get the crew home," said Kranz.[7]

What Went Wrong

Before NASA would send another crew into the inky blackness of space, it had to find out what had nearly killed this crew. Several months later, NASA figured out what the causes of the accident had been. An unlikely chain of human errors and technical issues caused the disaster.

In 1965, the engineers changed the spacecraft power supplies from twenty-eight to sixty-five volts. Such a change would normally cause engineers to change other components to the new voltage. But the people building the service module oxygen tanks were never told of the change. Each of the tanks contained a stirring fan and a heating element. There was a temperature-sensitive switch designed to shut everything off if the element got too hot. None of these components had been redesigned for the higher voltage. Two years before the *Apollo 13* flight, one of the oxygen tanks had been damaged. The tank was repaired and tested. It functioned properly. In the weeks before the launch, ground crews had difficulty draining the tank. Engineers decided that the problem was not serious. Replacing the tank would have delayed the flight.

Engineers believe when the stirring fan started, a wire sparked and the insulation caught fire.[8] The heat of the fire began raising the pressure. When the pressure was too high for the tank's thin walls, the tank exploded and damaged the other oxygen tank.[9]

Unlucky Number 13

Some people believe that the number thirteen is bad luck. Thirteen appeared in more than the mission number. The digits of the launch date, 4/11/70, when added together (4+1+1+7), total thirteen. The time of the launch at Mission Control in Houston was 1:13 P.M. Central Standard Time, which is 13:13 hours in military time. The mission was scheduled to enter the Moon's gravitational field on April 13. The explosion happened on April 13. Lovell saw the oxygen escaping into space

Immediately after the *Apollo 13* crew returned, NASA began looking into the causes of the explosion. The astronauts, however, were received as heroes. In this photo, from left to right, Fred Haise, Jim Lovell, President Richard Nixon, and Jack Swigert attend post-mission ceremonies at Hickam Air Force Base, Hawaii. President Nixon awarded the three men with the Presidential Medal of Freedom.

thirteen minutes after the explosion. Bad luck, however, had nothing to do with the accident. Human failures had caused it. Levelheaded thinking, teamwork, and months of training all helped in the safe return of the crew.

The *Apollo 13* crew had no idea that most of the world was watching, or listening, as the drama unfolded. "We didn't realize the complete magnitude of this flight," said Lovell, "until we got back home and started reading about it." The *Christian Science Monitor* reported: "Never in recorded history has a journey of such peril been watched and waited out by almost the entire human race."[10] The president summarized the reaction of many when he said, "The three astronauts did not reach the Moon, but they reached the hearts of millions of people in America and in the world."[11]

Aftermath

President Richard Nixon awarded the Presidential Medal of Freedom to the flight directors who helped bring *Apollo 13* safely home. He also awarded this medal to the three astronauts.

Jim Lovell never went back to the Moon. He left the lunar flight program and transferred to the new space shuttle program. He later retired from NASA and formed his own company. He wrote a book about his experiences that later became a movie. In 1995, President Bill Clinton gave him the Congressional Space Medal of Honor.

Neither Fred Haise nor Jack Swigert ever made it to the Moon. Haise became a test pilot on the space shuttle *Enterprise*. He later left NASA to become a president at Grumman Technical Services.

Jim Lovell wrote a book about his experiences during the *Apollo 13* mission. In 1995, the movie *Apollo 13* was released, which was based on Lovell's book. Bill Paxton (left), Tom Hanks (center), and Kevin Bacon (right) portrayed the three heroic astronauts in the movie.

Jack Swigert left NASA in 1978 to enter politics. In November 1982, he was elected to the U.S. House of Representatives as a congressman from Colorado. Before he was sworn in, he was diagnosed with a rare form of cancer. He died just a month later.

Ken Mattingly never got the German measles. He later flew three spaceflights: on *Apollo 16* as command module pilot, and as the spacecraft commander on space shuttles *Columbia* in June 1982 and *Discovery* in January 1985.

The Future of the Space Program

When *Apollo 11* landed on the Moon in 1969, NASA had planned to send at least nine more missions to the Moon. After the near tragedy of *Apollo 13*, Congress questioned the need for so many trips to the Moon. Nine months later, *Apollo 14* lifted off with redesigned oxygen tanks and other changes. By the end of 1972, *Apollo 17*, the sixth and last of the lunar landing missions, had been completed.

The last *Apollo* flight took place in July 1975. The *Apollo-Soyuz* mission was the first manned spaceflight conducted jointly by the United States and the Soviet Union. Although they were bitter Cold War enemies, the two countries worked together peacefully. The two spacecrafts docked and conducted experiments. The "Age of *Aquarius*" was over. The new age of the space shuttle and the creation of an International Space Station had dawned.

However, the *Apollo 13* accident served to remind NASA and the public that manned spaceflight was not routine or safe. The same lesson had to be learned again sixteen years later. On January 28, 1986, the space shuttle *Challenger* and all seven of its crew were lost shortly after launch.

On February 1, 2003, the world lost shuttle *Columbia* on reentry. That accident was determined to be caused by a piece of insulation that fell from one of the wings upon takeoff. These disasters serve to remind us no matter how commonplace shuttle launches seem to the casual observer, they are dangerous. The men and women who risk their lives are aware of the dangers and willingly take them for the benefit of all humankind.

Chapter Notes

Chapter 1. Danger and Disaster

1. Gene Kranz, *Failure Is Not an Option* (New York: Simon & Schuster, 2000), p. 308.

2. Edgar M. Cortright, Director, "Apollo's Expeditions to the Moon," July 28, 1975, <http://www.hq.nasa.gov/office/pao/History/SP-350/ch-13-1.html> (October 13, 2003).

3. Ibid.

4. Jim Lovell and Jeffrey Kluger, *Lost Moon: The Perilous Voyage of Apollo 13* (New York: Houghton Mifflin Company, 1994), p. 94.

5. Ibid., p. 95.

6. Roger D. Launius and Steve Garber, "Detailed Chronology of Events Surrounding the Apollo 13 Accident," *Apollo 13 Chronology*, May 29, 2001, <http://www.hq.nasa.gov/office/pao/History/Timeline/Apollo13chron.html> (October 13, 2003).

7. Kranz, p. 311.

8. Ibid., p. 314.

9. Lovell, p. 117.

10. Ibid., p. 113.

Chapter 2. Liftoff

1. Gene Kranz, *Failure Is Not an Option* (New York: Simon & Schuster, 2000), p. 308.

2. Edgar M. Cortright, "Apollo Expeditions to the Moon," July 28, 1975, <http://www.hq.nasa.gov/office/pao/History/SP-350/ch-13-1.html> (October 13, 2003).

3. "Apollo XIII," n.d., <http://www.mcn.org/Apollo13/Apollo13.html> (October 13, 2003).

4. Robert Godwin, ed., *Apollo 13: The NASA Mission Reports* (Ontario, Canada: Apogee Books, 2000), pp. 38–39.

5. Cortright, "Apollo Expeditions to the Moon."

6. Ibid.

Chapter 3. Saving the Crew

1. Gene Kranz, *Failure Is Not an Option* (New York: Simon & Schuster, 2000), p. 311.

2. Robert Godwin, ed., *Apollo 13: The NASA Mission Reports* (Ontario, Canada: Apogee Books, 2000), pp. 102–103.

3. Jim Lovell and Jeffrey Kluger, *Lost Moon: The Perilous Voyage of Apollo 13* (New York: Houghton Mifflin Company, 1994), p. 104.

4. Edgar M. Cortright, "Apollo Expeditions to the Moon," July 28, 1975, <http://www.hq.nasa.gov/office/pao/History/SP-350/ch-13-3.html> (October 13, 2003).

5. Lovell, p. 287.

6. Kranz, p. 12.

7. Cortright, "Apollo Expeditions to the Moon."

8. Kranz, p. 316.

9. Ibid., p. 322.

10. Cortright, "Apollo Expeditions to the Moon."

11. Godwin, p. 110.

12. Lovell, p. 76.

13. Cortright, "Apollo Expeditions to the Moon."

14. Godwin, pp. 113–114.

15. "Apollo 13 'Houston, we've got a problem.' Page 15," *Space Educator's Handbook*, n.d., <http://www.jsc.nasa.gov/er/seh/pg15.htm> (October 13, 2003).

Chapter 4. The Long Journey Home

1. "Apollo 13 'Houston, we've got a problem.' Page 15," *Space Educator's Handbook*, n.d., <http://www.jsc.nasa.gov/er/seh/pg15.htm> (October 13, 2003).

2. "Apollo 13 'Houston, we've got a problem.' Page 17," *Space Educator's Handbook*, n.d., <http://www.jsc.nasa.gov/er/seh/pg17.htm> (October 13, 2003).

3. Eric M. Jones, "Apollo 13 Transcript," *Apollo 13 Lunar Surface Journal*, 1995, <http://www.hq.nasa.gov/alsj/a13/a13.html> (October 13, 2003).

4. Gene Kranz, *Failure Is Not an Option* (New York: Simon & Schuster, 2000), p. 327.

5. Edgar M. Cortright, "Apollo Expeditions to the Moon," July 25, 1978, <http://www.hq.nasa.gov/office/pao/History/SP-350/ch-13-4.html> (October 13, 2003).

6. Kranz, p. 328.

7. Cortright, "Apollo Expeditions to the Moon."

8. Ibid.

9. Cortright, "Apollo Expeditions to the Moon."

Chapter 5. Preparation for Reentry

1. Gene Kranz, *Failure Is Not an Option* (New York: Simon & Schuster, 2000), p. 259.

2. "Apollo 13 'Houston, we've got a problem.' Page 17," *Space Educator's Handbook*, n.d., <http://www.jsc.nasa.gov/er/seh/pg17.htm> (October 13, 2003).

3. Edgar M. Cortright, "Apollo Expeditions to the Moon," July 25, 1978, <http://www.hq.nasa.gov/office/pao/History/SP-350/ch-13-5.html> (October 13, 2003).

4. Jim Lovell and Jeffrey Kluger, *Lost Moon: The Perilous Voyage of Apollo 13* (New York: Houghton Mifflin Company, 1994), p. 316.

5. Robert Godwin, ed., *Apollo 13: The NASA Mission Reports* (Ontario, Canada: Apogee Books, 2000), pp. 35–38.

Chapter 6. Reentry

1. Gene Kranz, *Failure Is Not an Option* (New York: Simon & Schuster, 2000), p. 335.

2. Jim Lovell and Jeffrey Kluger, *Lost Moon: The Perilous Voyage of Apollo 13* (New York: Houghton Mifflin Company, 1994), p. 331.

3. Ibid.

4. Kranz, p. 336.

5. Lovell, p. 333.

6. Edgar M. Cortright, "Apollo Expeditions to the Moon," July 25, 1978, <http://www.hq.nasa.gov/office/pao/History/SP-350/ch-13-5.html> (October 13, 2003).

7. Kranz, p. 333.

8. Lovell, p. 351.

9. Eric M. Jones, "Apollo 13 Transcript," *Apollo 13 Lunar Surface Journal*, 1995, <http://www.hq.nasa.gov/alsj/a13/a13.html> (October 13, 2003).

10. Cortright, "Apollo Expeditions to the Moon."

11. "Apollo 13 'Houston, we've got a problem.' Page 25," *Space Educator's Handbook*, n.d., <http://www.jsc.nasa.gov/er/seh/pg25.htm> (October 13, 2003).

Glossary

carbon dioxide—A colorless gas produced by the decay of organic substances. Human beings also give off carbon dioxide when they breathe. Too much carbon dioxide in a confined area will cause a person to suffocate.

command module (CM)—On the *Apollo* spacecraft, it contained the crew compartment, controls, many of the spacecraft's systems, and the heat shield.

fuel cell—A device that uses chemicals, such as hydrogen and oxygen, to create a reaction that gives off energy to power a machine, such as a spacecraft.

heat shield—The surface that covered the reentry side of spacecrafts. Parts of the surface were designed to burn away. This carried heat away and prevented heat from building up on the spacecraft.

lunar module (LM)—The *Apollo* spacecraft designed to land on the Moon. It also allowed the astronauts to blast off the Moon and to redock with the command module.

Saturn V rocket—The large rocket used to launch the *Apollo* astronauts on their voyages to the Moon.

service module (SM)—Attached to the command module, it contained the propulsion system and the oxygen and hydrogen fuel.

trajectory—The given path of a moving object through space.

Further Reading

Books

Goldberg, Jan. *James Lovell: The Rescue of Apollo 13*. New York: Rosen Publishing Group, 2004.

Hilliard, Richard. *Lucky 13: Survival in Space*. Honesdale, Pa.: Boyds Mills Press, 2008.

Pierce, Alan. *Apollo 13*. Edina, Minn.: ABDO Publishing, 2005.

Pyle, Rod. *Destination Moon: The Apollo Missions in the Astronauts' Own Words*. New York: HarperCollins, 2005.

Thimmesh, Catherine. *Team Moon: How 400,000 People Landed Apollo 11 on the Moon*. Boston: Houghton Mifflin, 2006.

Internet Addresses

NASA: *Apollo 13* Mission
    <http://science.ksc.nasa.gov/history/apollo/apollo-13/apollo-13.html>

Smithsonian National Air and Space Museum: *Apollo 13*
    <http://www.nasm.si.edu/collections/imagery/apollo/as13/a13.htm>

Lunar and Planetary Institute: *Apollo 13* Mission Overview
    <http://www.lpi.usra.edu/lunar/missions/apollo/apollo_13/overview/>

Index